JESUS AND ME

JESUS AND ME

ONE CHILD'S FRIENDSHIP WITH THE SON OF GOD

JOSHUA CARTWRIGHT

Jesus and Me: One Child's Friendship with the Son of God
Copyright 2019 © Joshua Cartwright
ISBN: **978-1-5272-4197-8**

All rights reserved. This book or parts thereof may not be reproduced in any form, stored in any retrieval system, or transmitted in any form by any means—electronic, mechanical, photocopy, recording, or otherwise—without prior written permission of the publisher, except as provided by United Kingdom copyright law.

This book is a work of fiction quoting passages from the Holy Scriptures.
Some characters and events in this book are fictitious. Any similarity to real persons,
living or dead, is coincidental and not intended by the author.

Scripture quotations from various Bibles including the Berean Bible, Holman
Christian Standard version, the New International Version, and the Amplified
Bible.

Publisher: **Throwbox Innovation Studios**, 99 Gardenia Avenue, Luton, Bedfordshire, England, UK LU3 2NR

Tel: 07882327490

Email: throwbox@mail.com

Artwork by Lone Animator
First printing 2019

SPECIAL THANKS TO:

MICHAEL & RONNAY RADFORD

MEL WITTER

IAN YOUNG

TABLE OF CONTENTS

WHERE JESUS AND IMMA LIVED 7

INTRODUCTION - NOTE TO PARENTS 8

BIBLICAL WORDS USED IN THIS BOOK 11

LET THE LITTLE CHILDREN COME TO ME 12

THE GOOD SAMARITAN 18

THE FEEDING OF THE FIVE THOUSAND 24

I AM THE BREAD OF LIFE 34

THE RAISING OF LAZARUS 41

JESUS ENTERS JERUSALEM ON A DONKEY 50

JESUS CLEARS THE TEMPLE 57

PENTECOST/FEAST OF HARVEST 65

GAMES CHILDREN PLAYED 76

ABOUT THE AUTHOR 81

WHERE JESUS AND IMMA LIVED

INTRODUCTION - NOTE TO PARENTS

It is my heart's desire that every child who reads this book will understand that Jesus truly loves them, and He is their friend (Matthew 19:14).

This little collection of stories imagines what it might have been like for a child who regularly came into contact with Jesus. Imma (a Hebrew girl's name meaning 'mother') lives in Bethany and Jesus would have passed through there to visit friends on His way to Jerusalem from Galilee, via Samaria or Jericho.

I have gently rearranged the timings of some Biblical events to help Imma encounter Jesus more easily - to my delight this method is similar to the one used to write the Gospels.* I've also tried to make the descriptions of Imma's surroundings as historically and culturally realistic as possible without boring the reader! I have also used some Hebrew and Aramaic terms translated into English ('Shalom,' for instance meaning 'peace') to add a flavour of authenticity.

Near publication, I found new research that suggested formal education - especially for girls - 'probably' didn't exist until after the time of Jesus; but I decided to keep the mention of 'school' in the story as it helps to demonstrate Imma's character and is relatable to the modern reader.

This is a work of fiction but - as a Christian myself - I understand the deep desire to ensure that nothing is added to, or taken away from, Scripture. Therefore, to clearly show the difference between Holy Scripture and the story I created - the words of Jesus are coloured in blue and the words I wrote are in black.

May you and your child be blessed with knowing Him more deeply.

JOSHUA ABRAHAM PAUL CARTWRIGHT

*Scholarly research has shown that ancient oral storytellers often told events in different orders depending on the people they were talking to, and particular theme or message they wanted to emphasize. This may explain why events are recorded in different orders in the gospels - it's not a mistake - just a different style of reporting and teaching.**

Jesus also taught in many towns and villages. Therefore, it is reasonable to assume He may have taught the same things in many different places. Please keep this in mind as you read parts of Scripture that has been combined from different places.

**Source: *The Jesus Legend: A Case for the Historical Reliability of the Synoptic Jesus Tradition* by Paul R. Rhodes Eddy

If you would like to receive a classroom-friendly First-Century Fact-Sheet about how Imma and her family would have lived, please visit:

www.jesusandmebook.com

Join the mailing list for book announcements, colouring sheets and other great free stuff!

BIBLICAL WORDS USED IN THIS BOOK

- **ABBA** = HEBREW FOR 'FATHER'

- **ADONAI** = HEBREW MEANING 'LORD' (USED IN JESUS' TIME INSTEAD OF YAHWEH)

- **ALEF-BET** = THE JEWISH ALPHABET

- **BETH-LEHEM** = BIRTHPLACE OF JESUS, MEANS 'THE HOUSE OF BREAD' AND 'THE HOUSE OF FIGHTERS'

- **BET SEFER** = JEWISH SCHOOL FOR 6-9 YEAR-OLD CHILDREN

- **ELOHIM** = HEBREW, A WORD FOR 'GOD'

- **GENTILES** = NON-JEWS

- **HASHEM** = HEBREW, MEANING 'THE NAME', REFERRING TO GOD

- **IMMA** = A HEBREW NAME MEANING 'MOTHER' AND THE WORD FOR 'MOTHER'

- **KYRIOS** = GREEK FOR 'LORD'

- **MASHIACH** = HEBREW FOR 'MESSIAH'

- **SHALOM** = HEBREW, MEANING 'HELLO, PEACE, PROSPERITY'

- **YAHWEH** = HEBREW - THE NAME OF GOD

- **YESHUA** = MEANS 'YAHWEH IS RESTORATION, SALVATION AND DELIVERENCE'

Let the Little Children Come to Me
Matthew 19:14; 18: 1-6

Imma had been grinding grain between two mill-stones. She was making flour so her mother could make bread. Her arms ached but she kept to it, knowing that it was essential for the family meal.

She heard the sound of children laughing in the road outside the door of her house. This was not unusual but …it sounded like there were a LOT of children out there. She could also hear the sound of gruff men's voices telling them off.

She brushed off her hands, opened the front door and stuck her head out.

Further down the road, Imma saw an ordinary looking man dressed in a rough-looking one-piece tunic and shawl with tassels. The local children were running around him as he played with them, pretending to catch them, and letting little ones hold onto his leg.

Imma loved to play, but she wondered "What's all the fuss about *this* man?"

Then, Jesus looked at her. His eyes were brown like those of most people she knew - but Imma had never seen such love and gentleness in a stranger's gaze.

Before she could stop herself she started walking towards Him. She didn't know why - but she just <u>had</u> to be near Him!

Suddenly, a large man stepped in front of her. He smelled of fish and sweat and he glared at her. "Leave the Master alone," he said. "Clear off, go-on!"

Imma stepped back, scared and unsure of what to do.

Then a gentle but firm voice said, "Peter…let the little children come to me and do not hinder them. For to such as these belong the kingdom of heaven."

Imma felt her courage return. She stepped around the man and ran towards Jesus. She briefly turned around to see the man called Peter (who must have been a fisherman by the way he smelled) watching her. She quickly stuck out her tongue at him…and - smack - ran straight into Jesus!

She quickly looked up - and saw a smiling face. He put His hands on her shoulders and said, "Who do we have here then?"

"Imma," she said and then, remembering her manners, she said, "Imma, Rabbi."

He bent down and whispered to her, "My friends call me Yeshua."

He placed His hand on her head and blessed her.

While she was standing next to Him little Ignatius, whose parents came to buy pottery from Imma's mother, also came up for a blessing. He beamed as Jesus prayed over him, and told Jesus, "I want to be just like you."

"That's the idea," said Jesus.

Peter came over. "Master, these children are always around you. Why are they so important in the Kingdom of Heaven? Will they be such great leaders in it at such a young age?"

Imma could tell he wasn't being serious.

Jesus stood up with His hand still on the head of little Ignatius. "Truly, I tell you, unless you change and become like little children, you will *never* enter the kingdom of heaven. But…if you take on a lowly position like these children you will be the greatest in the kingdom of heaven."

Peter nodded. "And Peter," said Jesus, "Whoever welcomes one such child in my name, welcomes me.

"If anyone…," and He paused… "*anyone* causes one of these little ones who believes in me to stumble it would be better for them to have a large millstone hung around their neck and be drowned in the depths of the sea."

Peter hung his head. "Yes, Rabbi," he said.

Imma was shocked. The Jewish people loved children but she'd never heard anyone say she was *so* valuable that someone who tried to hurt her faith would be better off dead!

She looked up at Jesus again, and for a moment drew closer to His side.

"Return to your mother," said Jesus to Imma. "She is expecting you."

"Yes Rabbi," said Imma and turned around and skipped back to her mother, her heart full of happiness.

THE GOOD SAMARITAN
LUKE 10: 25-37

One day, Jesus was in the courtyard of a local house belonging to Rabbi Yochanan. Many people from Bethany were there, and teachers of the Law of Moses from Jerusalem had also come to hear Jesus speak. Imma's father had brought her too.

One of the teachers stood up. Jesus turned to face him and the man said, "Teacher, what must I do to inherit eternal life?"

Jesus smiled, and said to him, "What is written in the law? How do you read it?"

Imma shot up her hand and made little 'me, me' sounds. Her father Yakob gently placed his hand over hers and pushed it down. "Let someone else talk this time," he whispered to her.

The teacher of the Law drew himself up, half-closed his eyes, and said, "You shall love Adonai your God with all your heart, and with all your soul, and with all your strength[1] ; and love your neighbour as yourself."[2]

Jesus replied, "You have answered correctly. Do this as a habit and you will live."

Imma looked annoyed. "I knew that since Bet Sefer," she muttered. Her father 'shusshed' her.

The teacher looked irritated. "And WHO is my neighbour?" he asked.

Jesus said, "A man was passing on his way from Jerusalem to Jericho when he encountered robbers who took all his possessions and beat him. He was half-dead when they left him."

"I've been on that road with Immah (mother) and some friends," said Imma quietly to the boy next to her. "It's scary and has lots of mountains."

Jesus continued, "Now by coincidence a priest was walking down that road and saw him, and passed on the other side."

Imma turned to her father. "Why, Abba? Why did he leave him?" Her father just looked at her, and then back at Jesus.

"Likewise, a Levite also came down to the place and saw him, and passed by on the other side of the road."

"I've got it," exclaimed Imma. "He left him because he's a Leave-ite!"

Several of the temple scribes turned and glared at her.

Jesus burst out laughing. "No, Imma," he said. "They are descended from the tribe of Levi."

"Did he leave someone too?" she asked. Even her father Yakob grinned at this.

Jesus returned to His story, "But a Samaritan who was travelling, came upon him; and when he saw him, he was deeply moved with compassion for him."

Imma saw some of the people from the temple whispering to each other when they heard this.

"He went to him and bandaged up his wounds, and he put him on his own donkey and brought him to an inn and took care of him.

"On the next day he took out two denarii (coins worth two day's wages) and gave them to the innkeeper, and said, 'Take care of him; and whatever more you spend, I will repay you when I return.'"

"That's really kind," said Imma to the boy. "Samaritans don't like us so much. They think you have to worship God on their mountain instead of at the temple."

Jesus turned to the teacher and looked him in the eye, "Which of these three do you think proved himself a neighbor to the man who encountered the robbers?"

The teacher gritted his teeth a little. He answered, "The one who showed compassion and mercy to him."

Jesus said to him, "Go and constantly do the same."

The man wasn't going to be rude to a Rabbi, but he felt embarrassed.

People would talk about him, and how the young Rabbi from Nazareth had taught *him* - an experienced teacher of the law - about mercy. Like he was some child!

He caught Imma watching him. He scowled and stomped off. Imma wondered why grown-ups had such a hard time learning new things!

Then she saw her neighbors Mary and Lazarus across the courtyard. She went over to them and chatted about how exciting it was to have Jesus in town.

SCRIPTURES MENTIONED:

[1] DEUTERONOMY 6:5
[2] LEVITICUS 19:18

THE FEEDING OF THE FIVE THOUSAND
Mark 6:30-44; Luke 9:10-17; John 6:1-15

Imma was trying to feed the squawking chickens in the courtyard of her house - and avoid an aggressive one that kept trying to flap up onto her grain basket.

She thought for a moment of kicking it - but remembered the Proverb her Abba had taught her, "A righteous man is kind to his animals".[1] She sighed, and wondered if the animals had been commanded to be kind back to people!

Imma's mother called out, "Imma, we are leaving now." She put the basket on a shelf, and went around to the front of the house.

The donkey was waiting, laden with provisions and a goatskin full of water. Her father lifted her onto it and took the bridle.

Imma's mother walked alongside her, and they began the descent down the hilly roads towards Jericho.

They were heading for a village called Bethsaida in Galilee, where Imma's grandmother lived. It was a long journey, over ninety miles, and they would have to sleep outside in tents on the way as it would take about seven days to walk!

Imma loved watching the stars with her father. She remembered what the prophet Isaiah had said:

"He stretches out the heavens like a curtain, and spreads them out like a tent to live in."[2]

The next few days were long, but there was so much to see. Fields of wheat and barley, vineyards, olive groves - once she saw some naughty boys sneaking into one and stealing olives before escaping from the workers there.

Imma's family had brought some food but when they wanted a snack they would pick a few ears of wheat, and rub the kernels between their hands until the seeds came out. They tasted so good!

Imma wished they could also eat some of the juicy grapes growing on the hillsides. But the vineyards were surrounded by thorny hedges and often she saw men watching them from the tall towers built to spot thieves.

Sometimes she would walk and her mother would ride on the donkey. But she was with her family, and family was everything to a little Jewish girl.

Imma's grandmother was called Bernice, and when they got to her house at Bethsaida, Galilee, she was inside, seated at the table.

She greeted Imma's mother, saying, "Joanna, blessed is she that comes."

Joanna gave the traditional reply, "Blessed be she that sits," and they both laughed and embraced.

Yakob came in through the door and said, "Peace be to this house."

"Good day, Yakob," said Bernice.

"Why are there so many people on the road?" said Yakob. "I know it's nearly Passover but I have never seen so many at once."

"That preacher Jesus is here," said Bernice, "He's heading out to the plains of Bethsaida. People are following Him."

Imma was excited. "Can we go too, Abba?" she asked.

"Well," said Imma's father, "I did like the way He answered that teacher of the Law. Perhaps He will have something else to surprise us with."

Imma jumped for joy and grabbed her father's hand. "Let's go," she declared.

"Not so fast," Yakob said. "Let's put our travel things down and have something to eat and drink."

A little later, as they walked out of the village, Imma held her father's hand tightly. Once they passed the last house belonging to Simon the Leper, they joined a multitude of people: entire families, and men by themselves. Hundreds and then thousands of people were streaming towards one place.

To see Jesus.

The ground began to rise and in the distance, beyond the crowd on a slope she could see a figure in white, surrounded by 12 other men dressed in similar clothes.

When they got as close to Jesus as they could, they sat down. The grass was green and soft, as it usually was for a brief while during the season of Passover.

Then Jesus raised His hand and the crowd fell silent. It was an awe-inspiring thing - to feel over ten thousand people just *waiting…waiting* on the words of one man.

Then Jesus spoke. His voice echoed deeply around the place and it had <u>such</u> authority. Every word He spoke was true…and Imma felt like the Kingdom of Heaven was so near she could just turn around - and she would see it.

Jesus spoke of the beauty of God's reign, He taught about His forgiveness; He told Parables that weaved together God's Truth with events from the fields and villages they lived in. Nobody moved, even babies did not cry.

Hours went by and then Imma heard her stomach 'growwwwl'. She had been *so* engrossed in His Words, but now she needed something to eat!

It seemed the disciples were thinking the same thing. Imma saw them go up to Jesus and talk with him.

She saw Andrew, Peter's brother, pointing back towards Bethsaida - and Jesus shaking His head.

Jesus pointed at Andrew, and Andrew said something and shrugged his shoulders. Then he picked up a basket which Imma supposed must have contained some food put aside for Jesus.

Jesus took it, and immediately after the disciples walked off in different directions through the crowd.

The one named Judas Iscariot came in her direction shouting, "The Master says 'Gather together in groups of 50.'"

There was plenty of grumbling as people shifted around, stepping on others' feet and moving children. Imma kept her eyes firmly fixed on her father, as there were
so many people there she didn't want to get lost.

Judas stayed long enough to see that their group had come together, and then he moved on.

Once everyone was seated, they looked at Jesus again. He reached into the basket (now on the ground), raised some bread to Heaven and thanked Yahweh for it. He did the same with the fish - and then….

PAGE 30

Imma's mouth hung open. It was as if during the moment she blinked, someone had piled bread and fish up high on the basket Jesus held. But that was IMPOSSIBLE. She had *just* blinked - and then it was there!

From the 'ahhhh' sound the people were making it seemed they had all blinked too! The sound swept across the crowded plain like a wave crashing onto the shore of Lake Tiberias.

But no one seemed to mind where the bread had come from when Jesus instructed his disciples to start passing it out. That's when the *next* crazy impossible thing happened.

The basket had been put on the floor and Imma could see, bread and fish being passed backwards into the crowd. But the food just *kept on coming*. Dozens and dozens of barley loaves and endless fish were somehow being picked out of the basket and handed to helping hands.

This went on for over an hour. Soon, as far as the eye could see people were munching on the fish, and tearing and eating bread.

Jesus gave an instruction and the disciples picked up other baskets they had gathered together. The baskets were passed across the crowd and unused food was dropped into them.

When they were all returned to the disciples - there were twelve baskets piled high with leftovers.

A man, dressed like a Rabbi himself stood up, and took three steps backwards. With each step he bowed to Jesus, once to the left, once to the right, and one bow to the middle. This was the way the Hebrew people would leave the presence…of a King!

There was a gasp from the crowd. "This is the King of Israel," Imma heard someone say.

That thought was passed from group to group to group until there was an electric feeling in the air. Something was about to happen. *Everyone* could feel it.

Suddenly, Jesus got up. He left, walking in another direction, and from the angry voices that erupted in protest, the crowd were not happy about this. Many people stood on their feet and shouted after Him.

Imma felt disappointed. Jesus had just demonstrated that God was truly with Him. Why would He not lead His people?

Yakob saw her face and said gently to her "Jesus is obviously a prophet, Imma. He may even be the Messiah. But you must remember that prophets answer only to God - and many people do not like that."

Imma was quiet. She pledged in her heart to speak to Jesus the next time she saw Him and ask Him what He was thinking.

SCRIPTURES MENTIONED:

[1] PROVERBS 12:10
[2] ISAIAH 40:22

I AM THE BREAD OF LIFE
JOHN 6:35

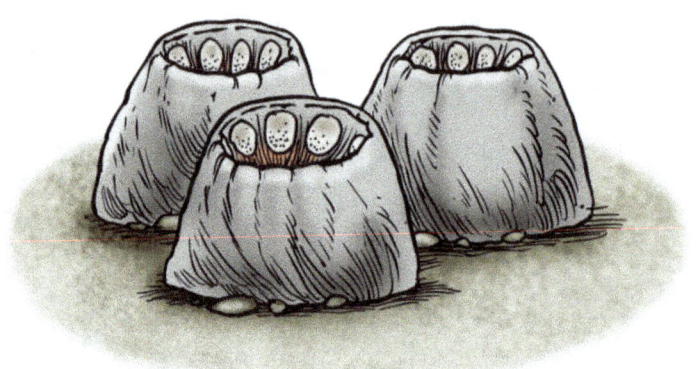

When Imma and her father got back from listening to Jesus, she felt very tired from all the walking.

Her father laid her on her mat next to a long goat's hair pillow. (When she was little she used to roll in her sleep so he had bought it to keep her still.)

She slept for a few hours - and when she woke up - her father was waiting. "Imma," he said in a serious voice, "Rabbi Yeshua is at his disciple Phillip's house. He wants to see you."

When she got to Phillip's house the disciples were outside. She said "Shalom" to them as she went inside. Jesus was standing there, and He smiled when He saw her.

"Imma," He said. "Peace be to she who comes."

"Peace be to He who waits in the house," she said, and then she felt like she wanted to blurt something out - but she kept quiet.

"I know you wanted to ask me something," said Jesus.

"I do," said Imma. She closed her eyes and said, "But I feel a bit scared."

"Fear not,"[1] said Jesus.

Imma opened one eye and looked at Jesus. "Isn't that what the angel of the Lord said to Gideon?"

"Yes," He said, and He winked at her.

Imma took a deep breath and slowly breathed out. Then she asked her question, "Why did you leave the plain?" she asked. "We want you to be our king and drive out the Romans."

Jesus got up without answering and walked about a bit. Then He said, "You know the prophet Isaiah spoke about the Messiah and called Him 'Prince of Peace'"?[2]

"Okay," said Imma.

"Do you think He could be a Prince of Peace if He raised an army and fought a war against the Romans?"

"I suppose not," said Imma, "but all our other kings were warriors. Even the songs of David say, 'For you have girded me with strength for battle; You have subdued under me those who rose against me.'"[3]

Jesus did not answer straight away but instead said, "Did you know I was born in Beth-Lehem?"

Imma shook her head.

"It's name means '*The House of Bread*' to many but it also means '*The House of Fighters.*'"

"So you *are* a warrior then?" said Imma.

"I have come to bring a sword,"[4] said Jesus, "but it's not the kind of sword *you* are thinking about. It is sharp enough to divide people - but my weapons are not of this world."

"I don't understand what you mean," said Imma. "But I do know the Messiah **will** be a King - and we've always had to fight to keep the Promised Land."

"Come to the window," said Jesus.

Imma walked over and looked up in the sky where Jesus was looking. He pointed up at the sun.

"Do you remember the story of how Yahweh made the sun stand still in the sky so that Joshua could win the battle?"

"Yes," said Imma.

"Do you think that the Elohim who did **that** cannot make another way? It is as the prophet Isaiah said, 'Behold I am doing a new thing...do you not perceive it?'[5]

"The solution, Imma, is '...not by might or by power but by my Spirit saith the Lord of heavens armies.'"[6]

Jesus sighed, "From the time of Saul my people have wanted a human king. They don't seem to have learned that that kind of king is not always good for them."

Imma thought for a moment. "But people were following you before you did this," - she searched for a word, "...miracle. They want to hear what you have to teach."

"The people following me now just want more loaves to eat," said Jesus. "They need to ask for the true bread that comes down from heaven."[7]

"What do you mean?" asked Imma. "I don't understand, you gave them bread to eat. I didn't see it fall from the sky though."

"I am the bread of life," said Jesus. "Whoever comes to me shall not hunger."[8]

"You don't look like bread," said Imma, giggling. "Where were you cooked?"

Jesus smiled, and then He looked serious. "Do you believe in Me, Imma?" He asked.

"Yes, Yeshua," said Imma. "And I love being near You and I want to follow You - but I don't understand what You are saying."

"Do you remember the Scripture 'Man shall not live on bread alone but on every word that proceeds from the mouth of God?'"[9] asked Jesus.

"Yes," she replied.

"So," said Jesus, "Do you think I am really talking about bread you can hold, bread that goes mouldy after a few days?"

Imma bit her lip and thought as hard as she could. She remembered when she was little and started school: the Rabbi had brought some cakes made into letters of the Alef-Bet with honey smeared on top, and let the children lick them.

Then she learned the Psalm - what was it? "How sweet are your words to my taste, sweeter than honey to my mouth…"[10]

Then her eyes opened wide, "Are you saying that your teachings are like…spiritual food?" she asked.

"Yes," said Jesus. "Exactly. I am feeding the people with spiritual food, and whoever believes in Me will never be thirsty[8], either."

Jesus paused, and then said, "Imma, you asked about a King. There is a King - and He will bring in the Kingdom of God."

"When?" said Imma, a little frustrated. "Where?"

"The Kingdom of God," said Jesus, "is not coming in ways you can see with observable signs. You won't be able to say 'Here it is!' or 'It's over there!' [but] The Kingdom of God *will be* among you."[11]

He pulled His shawl around His shoulders and walked to the door. "You are my littlest disciple, Imma," He said. "Never think you are small or insignificant. If you believe in Me, then when you are weak, you are strong.

"My Father has counted every hair on your head,[12] that is how much He cares for you."

He bid her 'good day', and went out in the night.

SCRIPTURES MENTIONED:

[1] JUDGES 6:23
[2] ISAIAH 9:6
[3] PSALM 18:39
[4] MATTHEW 10:34
[5] ISAIAH 43:19
[6] ZECHARIAH 4:6
[7] JOHN 6:58
[8] JOHN 6:35
[9] DEUTERONOMY 8:3; MATTHEW 4:4
[10] PSALM 119:103
[11] LUKE 17:20-21
[12] MATTHEW 10:30; LUKE 12:7

THE RAISING OF LAZARUS
JOHN 11:1-44

Imma knew when Mary and Martha, the sisters, were coming up the road by her house, Martha would be asking Mary questions like:

"Mary, did you close the sheep pen gate?"

"Yes, Martha."

"Mary, did you tell the baker we needed some extra loaves today?"

"Yes, sister."

"What about the oil for the lamps?"

"I got it yesterday, sister."

"That woman worries too much," thought Imma, and grinned to herself.

When they walked past her open front door, Imma counted to three. Then, as usual, there was Lazarus quietly walking five paces behind them. She often thought she caught a glimpse of a smile on his face.

Men usually walked in front of women, but Imma liked to imagine he walked behind them so he could amuse himself as his sister fussed and bothered.

So when Imma heard that Lazarus was sick, she felt sad. She wasn't worried, though, until Uncle Simeon came to the door and said that Martha had sent for Jesus.

Imma was excited to see her friend again. Jesus would make Lazarus well, she had no doubt.

Each day, before school, and after evening meal, she sat on the flat roof of her house looking towards the end of the road where Jesus would have to appear.

He didn't come the first day. He didn't come the second, and Imma heard that Lazarus was very sick. Her little heart was confused. Where was He?

Later that night, she heard crying and wailing coming from the house where Lazarus lived. She knew that meant he was dead, and she sobbed her little heart out.

The next day Imma saw the funeral procession come by.

Mary and Martha were walking at the front, and behind them were men loudly playing flutes. They were followed by women dressed in black who were wailing and shouting and shaking their fists.

Next came the men of the village, carrying the body of Lazarus in a wooden coffin. His body was wrapped in linen cloth with one piece covering his face.

Imma knew that for the next few days, Mary and Martha would not talk to her in the road - it was part of mourning. She wondered again where Jesus was.

On the sixth day, while on the roof, she saw a group of men in the distance. Soon, Jesus came into view. Imma was furious. She ran down the stairs on the side of the house and out into the road. She was planning to tell Jesus how mad she was with Him for not coming.

But before she could say anything, Martha ran past her. Martha stopped in front of Jesus and said "Lord, if you had been here my brother would not have died. But I know that even now God will give you anything you ask."

Imma was still feeling hot and angry. She looked around and saw that many people had come out into the road and were talking. Some were crying loudly and pulling at their hair.

She couldn't hear Martha well, so she made her way to the front to hear Jesus saying, "...he who lives and believes in Me will never die. Martha, do you believe that?"

Martha answered, "Yes, Kyrios. I know that you are the *Mashiach*, the one who was coming to the world."

"The Christ!" - Imma was shocked to to hear this said out loud again. She hadn't thought about it again much since her conversation with Rabbi Yeshua.

Once she had got over her disappointment that life was not going to change straight away, everyday life had been far too busy to fret about it.

The disciples arrived moments later. Thomas was looking around nervously. Imma heard him say to Phillip, "It's not safe here."

Phillip answered, "The Rabbi knows what He is doing" and Imma thought, "He sounds like grandma and Peter. He must originally come from Bethsaida as well."

Mary had come to Jesus as well, and said "Lord, if only you had been here my brother would not have died."

Then Imma saw an expression on the face of Jesus that she did not recognise. He looked angry and upset!

"Where have you put him?" Jesus asked.

"Lord, come and see," said someone in the crowd - and Jesus could not hold in his feelings anymore - He started crying.

Imma felt her heart soften. She ran to Jesus and stood in front of Him. She reached for His hand, and without talking, they both started walking with the crowd.

Mary led the way and they all walked to the edge of the city and into the area where the tombs were.

They stopped outside a cave with a large stone placed in front of it. Imma didn't like the graveyard. Her younger brother was buried nearby, and thinking about him made her sad.

"Roll away the stone," Jesus commanded.

Martha didn't want to. "Lord, he has been dead for four days. The smell will be terrible."

Jesus looked sternly at her. "Didn't I tell you you would see God's glory if you believe?"

Imma felt excited - and troubled - at the same time. What could Jesus *possibly* do here? But …she had seen the miracle of the multiplying bread and fish so… she shut her eyes tight - and believed.

Jesus shouted, "Lazarus, come out!" There was a scraping sound from the tomb, like linen on rock, and then Lazarus appeared at the mouth of the cave, still covered in the grave wrapping!

People shouted in shock, amazement, joy and fear. Many fell to their knees and started praising God.

Imma turned to Jesus, her eyes shining.

"Yeshua," she said, "now I know why you were angry. You were angry with death!"

Jesus smiled down at her and then gave the command, "Unwrap him, and let him go."

The walk back into the city was very different to the walk out.

People were shouting for joy, reciting the Shema, one of the most important prayers in Judaism:

"Sh'ma Yisrael Adonai Elohenu Adonai Echad"

which means:

"Hear, O Israel: the LORD is our God, the LORD is One."

Imma cast a glance back at Lazarus who was walking behind them. Her heart was full of wonder, but at the same time, she wasn't sure what to say to him.

What *do* you say to someone who had just been dead?

She heard someone call "Imma!" It was her father, who had seen Lazarus with Jesus - alive. His expression was the same as many of the people - he couldn't believe what he was seeing.

Imma went up to him and drew close to his side "Abba," she said quietly to her father, "What does it mean?"

"There has been no prophet in Israel for four hundred years," said her father. "And no one with such power from Adonai for longer than that.

"It means the Messiah is here - and soon everything must change for Israel and maybe the world."

Imma stayed quiet. She knew Jesus had said He didn't want to be a soldier king so she wasn't sure what to say.

"Can I go up to the roof, Abba?" she asked. "I want to pray."

Once the excited crowd had passed, it was quieter again. So she prayed, "Adonai, open the eyes of my heart so that I may see wonderful things in your word." And then…

"Please help me understand the One that brings your Word…He is my friend but He is kind of confusing to me!"

Then she opened her eyes - and went downstairs to help her mother prepare the evening meal.

Jesus Enters Jerusalem on a Donkey

Matthew 21: 1-11; Mark 11: 1-11; Luke 19: 28-40;
John 12:12-19

It was nearly Passover, and Imma and her family were preparing to go up to Jerusalem. This was the time when all Jews remembered Yahweh's rescuing of their people from the wicked Pharaoh of Egypt.

In about a week, Abba would take a lamb to a courtyard in the temple at Jerusalem and the priests would sacrifice it.

Later, they would take it home, sprinkle some blood on the doorpost of their house, and cook and eat the lamb. Imma loved having meals with her family, but she really didn't like the bitter herbs used to flavour this meat.

She knew it was Adonai's command to eat it, but it was really the thought of upsetting her mother that kept her from spitting one herb called *maror* - wild dandelion - into her hand!

It was the ninth of Nissan, a Saturday, and the Sabbath, so they had not been doing any work that day, as Moses had commanded them.

But, Sabbath had been over for a couple of hours when there was a knock at the door.

It was Thomas, one of the disciples of Jesus. After greeting Imma's father, he said, "Rabbi Yeshua would like to tell you he is going to Jerusalem tomorrow through the Eastern gate."

Then he reached under his shawl and brought out something. "Rabbi made this for you," he said and handed it to Imma.

It was a beautifully carved wooden horse. Imma gazed at it in wonder and when she found her voice she said, "Thank you, please tell him I love it."

"Rabbi was a carpenter and stone mason, you know," said Thomas. "He used to have a sign above his shop in Nazareth which said, 'My yoke is light'."

He paused for a moment, as if he was going to say something else. Then, he said "Good day" to Imma's father, and left.

The next day, they left late, as some of the goats had escaped from their pen and Imma had to help her father catch them. When they came back, their neighbour told them Jesus had gone ahead with His disciples.

Imma and her father set out along the road. As they walked closer to Jerusalem, they joined a seemingly endless procession of people on the road, flowing like a noisy human stream into, and out of, the Holy City.

The sides of Herod's temple loomed high above them in the distance, dominating the skyline ,and many people were looking up at it as they walked. It was a wonder - the dwelling place of Adonai on earth, or so her father said.

To pass the time, Imma played a game with her father of 'who is from where' - she was getting good at it - and she recognized caravan traders from Egypt, Syria,

Nabatea, Arabia, and Persia either by their appearance or by hearing snatches of their talk with each other.

Dotted here and there in the crowd were pilgrims and converts to Judaism, also from different places in the Roman Empire and, of course, there were Roman soldiers everywhere, especially the legionaries on duty.

She did not like these men. Not only were they very unkind, they also killed Jews. When she had to go across the city to the market she avoided looking at Golgotha, where the central beams of the crosses stood.

As they moved forward, there was a commotion in the crowd ahead. Excited voices passed back the news - Jesus was up ahead.

Imma asked her father, "Can I go on your shoulders Abba?" and he swung her up so she could see above the crowd.

In the distance, there was Jesus - riding on a donkey!

The roar from the crowd became almost deafening: and now people were climbing palm trees, and jumping up and breaking off branches. They were laying them down in the road and - even more amazing - taking off their outer cloaks and spreading them in front of the donkey!

Imma nearly cried with joy. When she saw Jesus on the donkey she was remembering the words of the prophet Zechariah:

"…your king is coming to you; righteous and having salvation is he, humble and mounted on a donkey, on a colt, the foal of a donkey.[1]"

"He IS the King," she cried out. "Hosanna! Hosanna! Hosanna in the highest heaven!"

Other people, including the disciples, were shouting similar things: "Hosanna to the son of David. Blessed is he who comes in the name of the Lord!"

A group of Pharisees approached Jesus. Imma saw them pointing at her and the disciples: "Teacher, tell your disciples to stop," they insisted.

Jesus laughed. He had to speak loudly over the noise of the disciples and the children … "I tell you," he said, "if they keep quiet the stones will cry out!"

He walked on and the angry faces were swept back into the crowd.

Imma held her hands to her chest.

"Jesus is the King!"

What would happen next?

SCRIPTURES MENTIONED
[1] ZECHARIAH 9:9

JESUS CLEARS THE TEMPLE

Matthew 21:12-13 ; Mark 11:15-17 ; Luke 19: 45-48

Imma was vexed. Yet again she had seen Jesus do something amazing - and then He walked away from it!

Again!

Yesterday, after He had triumphantly entered through the Eastern gate He'd gotten off the donkey and had a look around the temple courts.

Imma and her father had followed Him - but when He went through the Nicanor gate that led to the court of Israel (where only Jewish men were allowed to go) - she had to wait for Him.

He came out, and when He saw her He smiled. But instead of staying to enjoy - or even acknowledge the noisy praise going on around Him - He set off walking straight back to Bethany!

When Imma reached her house later that day, she did not see Jesus. But she knew He was nearby because, when she went up on the flat roof, she could occasionally see His disciples coming and going in the distance.

The next day, Imma and her father needed to be back in Jerusalem to pick up some special clay for her mother. The local trader they bought it from would have already removed stones and added sand to make it easier for her to work it.

Imma had a few copper coins called *leptons* in her hand and she asked her father if she could drop them in the temple treasury in the Court of Women.

Her father agreed, and they set out across the Mount of Olives.

Like the day before, they entered the Temple Mount through the Eastern gate which led into the court of the Gentiles. This was a massive area, open to almost everyone and used by almost everyone as it was a shortcut between the Mount of Olives and the main city of Jerusalem.

Imma could see many, many animals and birds which were being sold for sacrifice; also the tables of the money changers who charged to exchange local coins for the special ones needed to pay the Temple tax.

The noise was incredible - if any of the Gentiles had wanted to pray, they could not have heard themselves think!

Imma's saw her father shaking his head in disapproval at the scene as he guided her to the Court of Women. She was glad to leave some of the noise behind. There were signs at the entrance stating that only Jews were allowed in here.

So, under her father's watchful eye, she skipped over to the eleven trumpet-shaped contribution chests along the wall and dropped her offering in the last one. She said a short prayer to Adonai for her parents and ran back to him.

When they came out, she took a last look to her right - and saw Jesus. He was striding into the Court of the Gentiles. She caught sight of His face and He looked very determined - to do something.

It wasn't long before she discovered what! He reached a money changer's table and without pause, flipped it over. Swiftly moving onto the next one, He swept the coins and scales off the table. The outraged money changers leapt off their benches - before Jesus overturned those as well!

Those selling doves did not escape the eyes of Jesus either. Feathers showered the people as frantic doves flapped in all directions, their overturned cages broken open on the floor.

The temple guards, seeing the commotion, started making their way over towards Him.

Meanwhile, the traders had gathered around Jesus shaking their fists and shouting as He moved across the court, throwing down more tables and benches.

When the guards saw who was causing the trouble they stopped nearby.

"They're afraid the people will stone them if they touch Him," said Imma's father.

"Is it not written," shouted Jesus furiously, "'My house shall be called a house of prayer for all the nations'? But you have made it a den of robbers."[1]

It was hard to tell with all the noise, but it seemed like many of the people were cheering! By this time a larger group of priests in their white linen robes and tubular hats had gathered together - and they were glaring at Jesus with fire in their eyes.

This reminded Imma of a story her father had told her - told to him by Rabbi Eliezer ben Yaakov.

"The Levites also watch over the temple at night, Imma," he said with a twinkle in his eye. "But do you know what happens if one falls asleep?"

Imma shook her head. "Well, first the supervisor hits him with his stick…"

"And then?" said Imma.

Imma's father tried not to grin: "He can set the Levite's covering alight for not doing his job."

At the time, Imma had gasped and giggled.

But now she was thinking that the Levites at the temple looked angry enough to set Jesus' cloak alight!

Suddenly, she felt a bit scared for Jesus. He was just one man standing alone against all the priests. They were powerful people, everyone knew that.

But then she looked at Jesus - His face set like flint as He strode around - and she could feel His burning love for the *Hashem* of *this* temple and the world - and she loved Him for it.

"Go Yeshua," she yelled, surprising her father.

Jesus had made His point. He stared at the Levites and priests - and made His way back towards Imma and the Eastern gate.

An old man was next to Yakob. "Zeal for your house will consume me," he muttered to himself, quoting a Psalm of David, "but next comes the insults and the shame."[2]

Imma felt a chill run down her spine.

She took her father's hand and said, "Abba, come. We have to get the clay from the market for mother. You know how busy it gets near Herod's palace."

As they walked, Imma wondered why the priests would be so angry at someone who loved their God so much.

But one thing she knew:

Jesus wasn't ever boring - what was He going to do next?

SCRIPTURES MENTIONED:
[1] ISAIAH 56:7
[2] PSALM 69: 9-10

PENTECOST/FEAST OF HARVEST
ACTS 2:1-40

Jesus was dead.

It was late at night. Imma's father Yakob came over to where she was sleeping and put a hand on her. She woke up, looked at his face, and saw tears in his eyes.

She had seen her father get emotional when he praised Adonai, but these were not tears of joy. There was an aching sorrow in his face that she had never seen before.

"Rabbi Yeshua," - he paused - unable or unwilling to rush the words out, "Rabbi Yeshua is dead. The High Priest condemned him and the Romans crucified Him."

Imma set bolt upright, "No," she told her father. "No, no, no, **No**! He can't be dead. He's the Mashiach. You can't kill the Messiah."

Her father - for a moment - looked even sadder. "The Romans have killed many who called themselves 'king' in the name of their *Pax Romanus*, Imma.

"This is how they maintain," and he swallowed as if a bad taste was in his throat, "their 'Roman Peace.'"

"But He's different," shouted Imma. "You saw the miracles: He was sent by Adonai. How could Adonai allow it?"

"That's a question only Adonai can answer," said her father quietly. "But for a while, many people walking in darkness have seen a great light. Perhaps His teachings will endure through His disciples."

Imma started sobbing. "That's not enough for me Abba," she said. "I want my friend back."

Her father drew her close to him. "We all want that, my daughter," he said. "But He is dead now. You must accept that."

"Lazarus was dead too," said Imma, her face buried in her father's side. "He's alive now."

"This is true," said her father. "But never has a man brought himself back to life."

"Not yet," said Imma defiantly. Her father looked at the single oil lamp burning in the middle of the room and said nothing.

As the days went by, Imma did her daily tasks. But there was no joy in her heart. She did not sing as she swept the floors.

When her parents took her to Synagogue, she didn't want to listen to the teacher there, as he droned on and on about the law.

When *Rabbi Yeshua* had spoken at the Synagogue it was interesting. <u>He</u> made the scriptures come so alive that it was like He knew Adonai personally.

She knew that King Solomon had said, "Hope deferred made the heart grow sick"[1] - but what did you do when your hope was gone?

When she saw the Roman soldiers march through the village, she hated them, although part of her felt that Rabbi Yeshua would not have wanted her to feel this way.

But as time went by, the pain eased a little and she was able to pray again. She remembered Yeshua had called her His 'littlest disciple', and she resolved to remember Him by trying to follow His example in her life.

About five weeks after her father had told her the news, there was a quiet knock at the front door. A woman introduced herself to Imma's mother as Mary of Magdala, a fishing village on the Western shore of the Sea of Galilee.

"I was…I am a follower of Jesus. He asked me to bring a message to Imma," she said.
"He's dead now," said Imma's mother. "Why upset her further?"

Before Mary could answer, Imma's father came into the room. "Let her in Joanna," he said.

"Rabbi Yeshua took a special interest in our daughter; she can at least draw some comfort from His last words to her."

Mary stepped into the room and took off her sandals, and then her head-scarf.

Imma's father and mother took a little step back because Mary's face almost *glowed* with happiness.

"Imma," said Mary gently, "Rabbi Yeshua - is alive."

Imma's lip trembled "He can't be," she said, but inside her little heart, a spark of hope flared up.

"I have seen Him," said Mary. "Peter, Thomas, Phillip - all His apostles have seen him, touched Him, and eaten with Him."

Imma rushed up to her. "Where is He?" she demanded. "I want to see Him now!"

"It doesn't work like that," said Mary. "He is risen now and He appears to us when He chooses.

"But He has told us to wait in Jerusalem for the power of the Holy Spirit to come."

She looked at Imma. "He wants *all* His disciples there."

Joanna took a step forward. "The Romans are looking for you," she said. "If they find us with the other disciples, we'll be arrested."

Mary nodded. "This is true. But Jesus said 'If you obey my teachings then you are truly my disciples. *Then* you will know the truth - and the truth will set you free.'[2]

"Don't you want to know the truth, Joanna? Don't you want to be free? Isn't Adonai's freedom what <u>all</u> our people most want?"

She looked at Imma's father. "If there is one thing I have learned, it is that Adonai's freedom does not depend on the things we see around us. Rabbi Yeshua said that one day even our temple will be gone - but He will be with us always."

Imma's father nodded. "Yes," he said. "Yes, we will be there."

"We meet at the Feast of Harvest," said Mary. "We will tell you where nearer the time."

At the Feast of Harvest, thousands more people than usual came into Jerusalem to celebrate.

From the upper room of the house at which they were meeting, Imma could see the southern side of the Temple. There were pools called *miqva'ots* which were used by pilgrims before they entered the temple. There were long lines of people waiting to go under, and up out of the water so they would be clean in the presence of Adonai.
All the believers were praying together in Aramaic:

"Avvon d-bish-maiya, nith-qaddash shim-mukh…"

"Our Father - who art in heaven…"[3]

Suddenly the room began to shake. Imma held onto the window frame!

From nowhere, flames of fire burst into the air and stretched around the room like long pieces of burning silk. The rushing sound was like a storm over the Sea of Galilee, whooshing and flapping like a boat-sail in the wind.

The fire separated into individual clumps of flame - Imma thought it was like a small bush burning above each of the apostles - and then it descended onto them.

But there was no shouting in pain, no fear. The flame ran off them like water and disappeared. There was a moment's silence, heavy with wonder, and then each man started talking in a strange language.

Imma recognised some of the languages being spoken from the 'who is from where' game she played with her father. But she knew it was unlikely that Peter could speak Sumerian or Thomas spoke Elamite!

It was the hand of God, the same Holy Spirit that had fallen upon King Saul all those hundreds of years ago, now fallen upon the apostles.

Imma could feel the presence of her Friend. Tears sprang to her eyes, but this time - tears of joy, and she smiled until her face ached. He had not left her alone.

The Divine power that lived in Yeshua now sprang to life in the apostles - even in Peter - loud, brash, impulsive man that he was, now touched and transformed by the hand of God.

Imma looked out the window. A massive crowd had gathered outside the house. They had heard the rumbling and the wind and now could hear God being praised in their own languages!

Peter came out the house first, striding through the crowd and
making for the cleansing pools. He stood on the steps up to the temple and started speaking.

He told the crowd about Jesus. He told them who He was and how they were responsible for His death. It did not matter that many of them had not been in Jerusalem - all the people of Israel felt responsible for the death of their Messiah.

The people were cut to the heart. "What must we do, brother?"

"Change your minds about the direction of your lives," he said, "and be immersed, every one of you, in the name of Jesus Christ for the forgiveness of your sins. And you shall receive the gift of the Holy Spirit. This promise is for you and your children and for all who are far off - for all whom the Lord our God will call."[4]

Imma looked at her father. "Go," he said, and she ran downstairs and across to the pools. "I want to receive the Holy Spirit," she announced.

Peter bent down to her, "And so you shall, Imma," he said. "Rabbi Yeshua knows that you will lead many people to Him."

Imma smiled, and walked down the steps into the pool…

On that day about 3000 people were added to the number of believers. Many more were to follow…

From that day, Imma and her parents lived as part of the community of believers, praising God and leading others to follow Jesus. She had many adventures, but she always held onto something Jesus had said to the apostles "For I am with you always until the very end of the age…"(Matthew 28: 18-20)

You see, children have the heart to believe and follow Jesus as He commands. They are delighted to please Him - and this is something many adults can learn from (keep that part secret!).

This is why we are all commanded to be like little children - like YOU - at heart when we follow Him.

SCRIPTURES USED
[1] PROVERBS 13:12
[2] JOHN 8:31-32
[3] MATTHEW 6:9-13
[4] ACTS 2:39-45

***

I hope the story of Imma inspires you to grow and keep your faith in Jesus - and to follow Him no-matter what happens in your everyday life. He is the way, the Truth, and the Life. You <u>will</u> come to God the Father - through Him.

God bless you,

JOSHUA ABRAHAM PAUL CARTWRIGHT

GAMES CHILDREN PLAYED

Children of every age love to play! Jewish children in the time of Jesus were just like you - and here are some of their games.

OUTSIDE GAMES

One game was like Hopscotch, played on the flat roof of a house that had a wall around it - to stop people falling off! Another game was played with 12 pebbles and called GAP - see how to play on page 79.

TOYS

Did you know that whistles, hoops, spinning tops and even carved animals-on-wheels have been found? Girls had dolls and model animals made of clay or pottery.

BOARD GAMES

Kids played games that we would recognise as chequers/draughts!

MAKE-BELIEVE

Children would copy what they saw the adults doing. Jesus talks about children playing flute and dancing to the music - this would have happened at a wedding. They also pretended to be the people who were crying at a funeral.

We have our Christmas Nativity plays and Thanksgiving. Jewish children would also act out famous events from the Old Testament such as the crossing of the Red Sea or David and Goliath! I'm sure Jesus would have played David!

WRESTLING

Yes. Jesus probably would have taken part in wrestling! No hitting each other with chairs like the wrestling you see on TV - this wrestling was to build strength and confidence, not to hurt people.

HOW TO PLAY THE JEWISH GAME OF 'GAP'

Find 12 small stones - make sure they are not sharp or ask your parent to buy some decorative stones that get placed in plant pots.

Get someone to gently throw the stones in the air - and see how many you can catch of the back of your hand.

The winner is the person who catches the most stones!

REVIEWS

Thanks for reading!

If you enjoyed this book **I'd be very grateful if you'd post a short review on Amazon**. Just go to www.amazon.com or www.amazon.co.uk (or your country's Amazon) type in 'Joshua Cartwright' and click on the cover of *Jesus and Me: One Child's Friendship with the Son of God*.

Your support really does make a difference - we are helping each other and our children grow in faith - what could be more important? I read all the reviews carefully so I can get your feedback, and make my books even better.

May God bless you richly.

Joshua

ABOUT THE AUTHOR

Joshua Cartwright has been a Christian for over 21 years and has loved reading about Biblical lands and customs for almost that long.

When his little daughter, Seraphina, aged 8, asked him to put her inside the nightly Bible stories - the seeds of this book were sown. A few months later the Holy Spirit told him it was time to start writing.

Joshua remembers that the leader of the first church he attended taught it was important to try and imagine yourself in the Scriptures as they happened.

All these influences have come together to create *Jesus and Me*.

Joshua is the author of 12 other books including: *The Granny JJ Adventures, The Girl who Took FOR-Ever!* and the adult psychology book *Your Mind is a Liar*.

God bless you,

Joshua

Other books by Joshua Cartwright
Available on Amazon

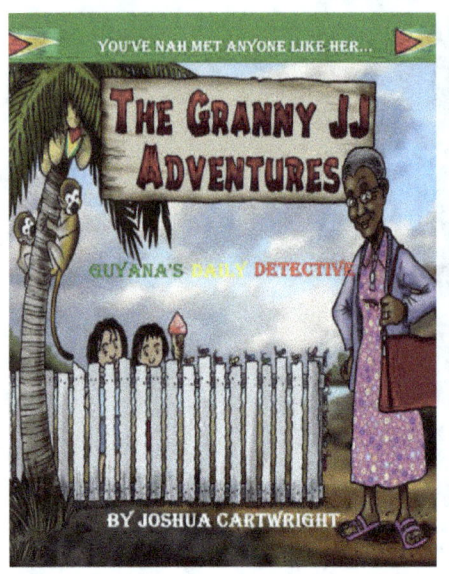

Join the mailing list at www.jesusandmebook.com

www.ingramcontent.com/pod-product-compliance
Lightning Source LLC
Chambersburg PA
CBHW051354070526
44584CB00025B/3756